COAST TO COAST
IN THE MIDDLE AGES
(You must be Bonkers!)

This walk is dedicated to the memory of our daughter Lisa's horse "J.J.",
who had to be put to sleep two days before we started the walk.
She was our friend.
She was a lovely horse.

ACKNOWLEDGEMENTS

I would like to say "thank you" to Derick for his chauffeur duties, to Alma, who typed my original manuscript and finally to Eric, for going with me without complaining (much).

COAST TO COAST
In the Middle Ages
Copyright © 2002 Lesley Bell

Lesley Bell has asserted her right under the Copyright, Designs and Patents Act. 1988 to be identified as the author of this work

This book is sold subject to the condition that it shall not, by way of trade or otherwise, be lent, resold, hired out, or otherwise circulated without the publisher's prior consent in any form of binding or cover other than that in which it is published and without a similar condition including this condition being imposed on the subsequent purchaser.

British Library Cataloguing In Publication Data
A catalogue record for this book is available from the British Library

ISBN 0 9537203 3 0

Published by:
P3 Publications
13 Beaver Road,
Carlisle,
Cumbria,
CA2 7PS
Website: www.p3publications.com
Tel: 01228 543314

Printed in the UK by:
Ink Truck
Lorne Crescent
Carlisle
CA2 5XW

THE BEGINNING

"You must be bonkers!"

These were the parting words from Eric's 88 year old Mum, on our visit to her just before setting out on our Coast to Coast walk. As it turned out, there were several occasions over the following two and a half weeks when we wholeheartedly agreed with her.

Not daft, Eric's Mum.

I'd been wanting to do this walk for about 6 years, and I'd gradually acquired everything necessary, maps, Wainwright's little red guide book, accommodation guide, compass, plasters. In fact, I'd had the accommodation guide for so long I'd declared it out of date, and bought another one.

I'd even had a practice, assembling the minimum that I thought I'd need, then squashing it all with difficulty into my rucksack, and finally hoisting it on to my back; to see if I fell over backwards.

Fortunately, I didn't, but my knees did buckle slightly.

I knew that Eric had doubts over whether his arthritic body would cope, and certainly it wouldn't have done six years ago, as his toes were too bad then. That problem was solved in 1993 when he had both big toe joints fused; fortunately not to each other. The few years after that seemed to be dogged with family crises, and there was never enough free time to even consider doing it.

We knew we didn't want to do it in summer, as the available accommodation would be overstretched and the

THE BEGINNING

temperatures might be too warm. Winter was definitely out because of the grim weather. This left autumn or spring (quick, aren't I?). Generally we do more walking in winter, and therefore are probably at our fittest in spring. But spring for us was restricted to either March or April due to other holiday commitments, and those months in England can be, well, wet and/or snowy, and certainly wet underfoot.

So autumn it would be. October, when the weather was usually fairly settled, the ground at its driest, and the autumn colours beautiful, and we'd just have to get fit along the way.
With all this misguided optimism in mind, and as Eric had run out of excuses, we named a departure date in October 1998.

It's times like this when you need a good friend, as a brief phone call established that getting to St. Bees by rail from our home would take a whole day. Fortunately we have a good friend, Derick, who volunteered to drive us there.

We left home at 8.00 a.m. and had a trouble-free leisurely drive across the Dales and South Lakeland. When we reached Ravenglass, we treated Derick to lunch at the railway cafe there (highly recommended) and arrived at St. Bees at 1.30 p.m..

Stop! We've changed our minds!

DAY ONE - ST. BEES TO SANDWITH

Ominously, it was blowing a gale. The sea was very rough. St. Bees struck us as being a rather bleak place. It may not be quite the end of the earth, but on a clear day you can probably see it from there.

With some reluctance, and even more trepidation, we got our boots on and went down to the sea for Derick to take the obligatory "paddle in the sea" photograph. He then waved us off, got back in his nice warm car, and set off to drive home.

The obligatory "paddle in the sea" photograph

Day One: St. Bees to Sandwith

That was it, we were on our own.

At this stage I think I'll say a bit about our equipment. We both had good quality Meindl boots, which were fairly new, and Craghopper jackets and overtrousers - which weren't. We had decided to walk in shorts whenever possible, and I had also taken some breeches. We had cut the rest of our clothing to the absolute minimum, that being, basically, three sets of undies, T shirts and socks each, a thermal jumper, and one decent set of clothes for evenings.

We obviously had the necessary toiletries and nightwear, and a medical kit that would have enabled us to perform a small operation on someone, had we also had the skill. The only "luxuries" we had were the camera, some binoculars and a borrowed mobile phone and its charger. Even so, when all the other essentials were added to the heap, like maps, guide books, survival bags, etc. the packs weighed slightly over a stone. Now I know that might sound like a bag of feathers to the average army chap, but we weren't used to carrying it and, as the walk progressed, we found that by the end of the day it got to feel pretty heavy (Some allowance should be made here for middle age and infirmity).

We had also taken two "Trekking Poles" - high-tech. walking sticks. These seemed a bit pretentious to us at first, but they proved to be worth their weight in gold later.

So off we went along the cliff path. It was well trodden, as cliff paths are. The route, rather alarmingly, as we were supposed to be going east, started off going northwards, round St. Bees Head, for almost four miles. The going was made difficult by a very strong gusting wind blowing in from the sea, and the unfamiliar weighty packs making us top-heavy.
The path in places had been worn to one of those awkward grooves that are only wide enough for one boot.

Day One: St. Bees to Sandwith

Progress was as follows: Lift right foot.
Gust of wind blows foot sideways off path.
Struggle to get it back in groove, move forward one pace.
Lift left foot.
Gust of wind blows it across in front of you.
Plait legs, fall over.
Get up, lift right foot — etc.

In this manner we lurched along the cliff. It was a good thing that the wind was blowing from the sea and not towards it or the walk may have ended for us on day one.
The views, which were superb, took my mind off the difficulties. The sandstone cliffs were worn to fascinating shapes by the sea and wind, and distant views were to be seen up and down the coast.
The weather did the dirty on us with a heavy shower only half a mile from Sandwith, where we had booked a bed for the night. We arrived at our B&B, Spout House, at 4.00 p.m..

Our accommodation, surprisingly, was a self-contained flat with all mod. cons., very pleasant. I had discovered before setting out that the village pub (I only knew of one) had stopped doing food, so had asked our B&B lady, Mrs. Buchanan, to make us some sandwiches. After we had fed and spruced up a bit, we went out to sample Sandwith night life. On the way to the pub we used the mobile to let our friends and relatives know we hadn't given up yet, and also to book the next night's B&B at Ennerdale Bridge.
The lady with whom we booked, Sheila Sherwen, warned us that dirty deeds were afoot on the descent from Dent, a hill we would be tackling on day two. Apparently there had been some dispute over the coast to coast route, and signs had been turned; resulting in some walkers going a long way off-track. We resolved to be on our guard.
Then we visited Pub No.1. The place was in the process of changing hands, which might explain why it was

Day One: St. Bees to Sandwith

such a dismal hole. There were only three or four people in, and conversation died when we arrived. It reminded me of those Western films where everyone in the saloon stops playing cards to stare at the stranger.

We had one drink and moved swiftly on to the second pub which was much better. They had at least turned the lights on. So, with the fleshpots of Sandwith sampled, we emerged to find the street awash in torrential rain, and sprinted back to our flat, to prepare for an early start; breakfast at 7.30 a.m..

Rough seas off St. Bees Head

DAY 2: SANDWITH TO ENNERDALE BRIDGE

After the previous night's rain, we were pleasantly surprised that the weather was fine, and remained so all day, one of our few (as it turned out) completely dry days.

We left Sandwith just after 9.00 a.m.; the packs now slightly heavier as we had succumbed to the temptation of Mrs. Buchanan's packed lunches. From now on I had to work a bit harder at route finding. Up to now there'd been no problem. After all, any fool can follow a cliff path, but now I flexed my navigational muscles and stuck my nose to the map. Eric is no help when we're on foot. He's great on roads, but put him on a footpath and his directional sense has a lie-down and leaves it to me. He can't see a map without his glasses anyway.
Knowing how popular the Coast to Coast has become, I half expected to find a trail three yards wide blazed across the country. I was pleasantly surprised (most of the time) that this was not the case, and some effort had to be put in to follow the route. Although we had other maps with us, we were following the specialised Coast to Coast "strip" maps, and I was aware that the penalty for poor navigation would be that you fell off the map, if you strayed more than one mile off the route.

Sobering thought!

After a couple of miles the route went under a disused railway; which is now being used as a cycle route. We climbed up onto the track to take in a drink, and the view. There, in centre stage, and only about two miles away, was St. Bees; which was rather frustrating as we'd covered seven miles to get to that point. We stopped again about one and a half miles further on, just past Moor Row. We were both finding the rucksacks a bit heavy and it was a relief to take them off for a while. We set off again across a field, and at the end of it. I glanced down to check that we were on course.

The map wasn't hanging round my neck!

Day 2: Sandwith to Ennerdale Bridge

I'd left it at the last rest point; hung on a stile. I scampered back to get it. Fortunately, it was still there. I didn't fancy having to tell people we had to give up after eight miles because I'd lost the map!

Just past Sandwith with the Lakeland hills in the background.

When we reached the top of Dent Hill we had great views all round. St. Bees still looked irritatingly close to say we'd been walking for a day.

On the descent from Dent the path plunged into a fir forest. It was in this forest that we came across a dodgy signpost, suggesting we should go left, when the map I had said to go right. We decided to follow the map and consequently had no problems, and owed Sheila our thanks. When we emerged from the forest we lounged in the sun for a while, by the stream at Nannycatch Gate, before setting off up the valley by the beck.

Day 2: Sandwith to Ennerdale Bridge

It seemed a very long mile up the valley before we met the road to Ennerdale Bridge. When we reached Ennerdale Bridge we felt quite tired, and could only hope that we'd get better as the walk progressed.

Starting the descent from Dent

We began searching for our B&B, which according to our guide was near the pub. We spent some time looking in the area of the pub before discovering that there was another pub. Finally, after doing what we should have done in the beginning, i.e. asking a local, we found the right cul-de-sac and actually met Sheila at the entrance to it; she was just taking her dog, Red, for a walk.

Much to Red's disgust, she turned back to let us in.

Day 2: Sandwith to Ennerdale Bridge

We made some tea before soaking in a welcome bath, then fed splendidly at the Shepherds Arms. The mobile phone turned sulky and refused to pick up a signal, so we used the local phone box to give a report to home, and book the next bed.

We set the pattern for the rest of the walk by turning in at 9.00 p.m., 'cream-crackered,' and I felt to be starting with a cold. Oh dear!

Well, when we were in the pub, we saw a forecast for the following day on a blackboard. It read:

"Cloudy, rain at times, sometimes heavy.   Cloud base 500 ft."

This proved to be not wholly accurate as in fact it only rained twice, once from dawn to 2.00 p.m. and once from 2.15 p.m. till 6.00 p.m. Also, I think they'd got the decimal point in the wrong place when quoting the cloud base as, when we got up the following morning, it looked to be at 5 ft. to us.

We sat in Sheila's kitchen watching rain stream down the windows while Sheila cooked breakfast and told us horror stories of the floods in June. Apparently there was so much rain then that Coast to Coasters were having to turn back from the Ennerdale Valley route because they simply could not ford the raging torrents that were supposed to be mild pleasant streams. This gave us a good excuse to revise the day's route. I've never been a great fan of trying to navigate across mountain tops in thick mist, so we studied our alternative maps and opted for the super-cowards route. That was (no - not going home) following a bridle path which went over comparatively low ground, 1,500 ft., to Buttermere, and from there up the road over Honister Pass.

DAY 3: ENNERDALE BRIDGE TO ROSTHWAITE

So, we departed Sheila's warm house and reluctantly set forth in sheets of rain. We called at the Post Office to stock up on goodies and shared our plan with the Post Master. He thought we were very wise, which made us feel much better and less wimp-like.

We trampled two miles along wet roads to Whins farm and then started the ascent up the wet bridlepath. According to the map, we passed within 250 yds. of Floutern Tarn on the way, but we never saw it. Visibility was restricted to the immediate thirty yards of squelchiness. To say that it was wet underfoot would be an understatement in the extreme. Cumbrian horses must have webbed feet.

"There's supposed to be a tarn around here"

Day 3: Ennerdale Bridge to Rosthwaite

It wasn't long before I detected that approximately half of the available water was in my left boot. Shortly after, Eric found the other half in his right boot.
The trekking poles started to earn their keep, they were invaluable for fording streams and testing the depth of bogs. Although the path was a bit indistinct in parts, we didn't have any major problems navigating, it just seemed a long wet way.

Even the lane leading across the valley bottom to Buttermere village had grown considerably longer since we last walked along it. We eventually reached the haven of the hikers bar at the pub, and an embarrassing puddle formed around us as we disrobed.

We had some very expensive soup to justify our presence to the barman, and sneaked in turn to the loos to change our sodden socks for dry ones. I realised that I'd made a basic error by putting my gaiters on over my waterproof trousers, thus channelling all the water, which was running down my body, straight into my boots.

I rearranged my clothing to correct this.

Below Scale Force near Buttermere
(Blobs of rain on the camera lens)

Day 3: Ennerdale Bridge to Rosthwaite

Back in the bar, we got into conversation with a couple who, judging by their respectable appearance, were touring the Lakes by car. They probably thought we were mad.

It was still raining when we left the pub to do the remaining seven miles, but as we were trudging up the road past Buttermere Lake, it did actually stop. We had brief hopes of our gear drying off, but it started again fifteen minutes later, with renewed vigour. It is a long slog up the road over Honister, about four miles of steady ascent up to 1,000 ft., with water flowing in torrents down the road against us. It was not fun.

During our ascent, a car passed us and pulled into a lay-by about fifty yards further on. We wondered whether it contained the couple we had spoken to in the pub and whether they had stopped to offer us a lift. We decided that, if that was the case, we would heroically decline, which was perhaps as well, as before we reached it the car set off again. I think they'd realised what a mess we'd make in the back seat.

After what seemed a small lifetime, we reached the summit, to find, to my surprise, that the quarry there was being worked again, and, Oh Joy!, they had a sign out advertising the sale of tea and coffee. We had no need to consult each other before presenting our soggy persons at the counter, and spent as long as we could over two mugs of coffee. Outside, the wind and rain carried on relentlessly. Eventually, when we realised it would be impractical to spend the night there, we carried on. At least the rest of the day's walk had the decency to be downhill. With the bonus of travelling downstream, as it were, we made good time for the remaining three miles to Rosthwaite. The only point of interest on the way was when we saw a large frog *'swimming'* across the road. As we approached civilisation, we began to wonder whether the poor lady we were booked in with knew what she'd let herself in for, but we needn't have worried. When Margaret Cashen opened her door to two mobile puddles she couldn't have been more welcoming. "Oh, come in, come in, it won't harm anything, it's only water" she said cheerily.

Day 3: Ennerdale Bridge to Rosthwaite

We removed our boots by the door and were shown to a lovely room, leaving a trail of damp marks on the stairs carpet. We obeyed instructions to hand over all our sodden gear for Margaret to deal with. In what seemed a remarkably short time, she had fed us tea and biscuits, dried our waterproofs and rucksacks, and washed and dried all our dirty clothes.

I would like to nominate this lady for a medal.

During the evening, the sky finally ran out of rain, and we walked the short distance to the local for some food.
The pub wasn't very busy, and it was easy to eavesdrop on conversations of others there. There was a couple who were staying in a rented cottage. The literature describing their cottage referred to the gentle tinkling of the stream running nearby. The "tinkling stream" was now a furious mass of white water.

Mum's parting words were beginning to ring true.

When we left the pub, we still couldn't get a signal on the mobile, so we used the local box (again) to book ahead, and were tucked up in bed at 9.00 p.m.

One good thing, my cold had not developed into anything.

Bugger must have drowned!

Eagle Crag at the entrance to Langstrath

DAY 4: ROSTHWAITE TO GRASMERE

Strange stuff, British weather. We arose to a sunny, blustery day with just a few clouds scudding across the sky. For the first mile or two it was coats on, coats off, but then the clouds dispersed and the coats stayed packed away.

Wainwright describes the walk up Stonethwaite valley as a walk in heaven, he was right, it is. Everything was beautiful, waterfalls, trees, hills, autumn colours; all competing for our attention. They took our minds off the ever - steepening path, as we climbed past Eagle Crag, towards Lining Crag. The stony gully up to the top of Lining Crag was particularly taxing, being wet and slippery underfoot.
I wouldn't want to tackle it in icy conditions. The views from the top were wonderful and I took some photos while we got our breath back.

From that point on, the path, presumably along with all the "too numerous" cairns mentioned by Wainwright, had sunk without trace into an extensive peat bog.

I found the going particularly difficult, as Eric, showing his true chivalry, had sneaked off with both trekking poles while I was packing my camera away. I recognised what a great asset a pole was when I was trying to get across man-eating (and woman-eating) bogs without one. Eric must have picked up the venomous vibes I was transmitting as he finally waited for me to catch up after about a quarter of a mile (unless he was just unsure of the route and needed my guidance).

Looking south up Langstrath

Day 4: Rosthwaite to Grasmere

I needed guidance too. The written instructions told us to aim for an iron stanchion, but that wasn't very helpful as there was more than one to choose from. Despite everything we did get to Greenup Edge, and from there, as promised by A.W. in the trusty red book, Grasmere was indeed visible. Therefore there was no danger of us falling into the "Wythburn Trap" (also described in the Little Red Book). The Wythburn is a valley which tempts the walker to go down it north eastwards, and on a misty day the error would not be detected until the hapless walker reached Thirlmere instead of Grasmere.

At the second mini-summit of Far Easedale, we were battered by an almighty wind that seemed intent on blowing us to Grasmere in a matter of minutes. It was a great relief when we dropped down the valley a bit, shunning the 'Big Boys' route along the ridge.

On the way down, we met a party of three gents who were on the way up. They warned us of a hazard in the stream lower down. The middle stepping stone was, in fact, a dead sheep. Poor thing was probably a flood victim from the previous day.

Stonethwaite Beck, looking back towards Borrowdale

Day 4: Rosthwaite to Grasmere

The summit of Lining Crag

It was an easy trundle down to Easedale, and we soon found our Guest House, and went in through what proved to be the back door, next to the kitchens. It was a much bigger place than I had been expecting, as in the Coast to Coast accommodation guide they had only advertised as having four rooms. I noticed at least a dozen rooms as the lady who greeted us showed us to ours. She told us that it was the custom of the house to serve tea and home-made cakes in the lounge at 4.00 p.m.

We had arrived in good time for this, as the day's walk had been fairly short; at nine miles. In fact, we had time to nip down into Grasmere to do a bit of necessary shopping. When we returned we went in by the front entrance to our guest house and discovered that it was a Quaker guest house - interesting.

Day 4: Rosthwaite to Grasmere

We were in the lounge about ten minutes before the appointed tea-time and were able to observe the other guests gathering for the goodies. We concluded that a prerequisite of being a Quaker must be that one is over ninety years old, unless, of course, being a Quaker ensures longevity. The lounge started to take on an alarming resemblance to an old folks home as the guests gathered and compared notes on their day. One lady made up for the lack of a companion by talking to herself. Eric and I studiously avoided looking at each other, and a diversion arrived in the form of the tea trolley. Having partaken of the refreshments, we beat a retreat to our room, and performed our daily ablutions and laundry tasks.

Sourmilk Gill, Easedale

Day 4: Rosthwaite to Grasmere

That evening we went into Grasmere and dined in the public bar of the Red Lion. We found that we were still dependent on the public call box for communication, and began to wonder why we'd bothered lugging a mobile phone along with us, but I expect it was enjoying the ride.

When we got back to our guest house the other guests were all in the dining room having the evening meal. We felt quite tired so we went straight to our room. We set the alarm for 8.00 a.m. and got ready for bed.

Five minutes later the alarm went off. It was 8.00 p.m.

This incident gave us the giggles big-style. There we were, feeling that we were spending the night in an old folks home, yet they were still going strong downstairs and we were in bed at 7.55 p.m. That's what long-distance walking does for you.

37 miles done, only 153 to go.

DAY 5: GRASMERE TO PATTERDALE

Leaving Grasmere

Breakfast at the guest house was a very social, if slightly hostel-like, meal. We met some Quakers who were not only under ninety, but also very friendly. We had an interesting conversation over our cornflakes and learnt a little more about the guest house.

We left Grasmere at 9.50 a.m. to do the eight or nine miles to Patterdale in mixed weather of sunshine and showers. We crossed the A591 and started up the valley towards Grisedale Tarn, with Tongue Gill Force for company. We were overtaken by a walker and his Alsatian dog and passed a few pleasantries with them both.

Just where the paths split to go round the Great Tongue, a shepherd was working his dogs, bringing sheep down through the fields. We stood and watched them for a while. Working sheep dogs are fascinating. When it seemed that all the sheep were down, the shepherd sent one dog back to search the bracken on the higher ground and flush out any sneaky sheep. We could see the dog from where we were and he certainly made a thorough job of the search. How do they know what is required of them?

We carried on up the right hand path and it wasn't long before the rain came and we took shelter under some overhanging rocks. Further up the valley we could see the walker and Alsatian striding on, leaving us for dead it seemed. The shower moved on and so did we. As the weather brightened, the path steepened and our pace

Day 5: Grasmere to Patterdale

slackened. Eric was feeling particularly drained; he must have had Coast to Coast Fatigue Syndrome.

Our stops to admire the view became longer and more frequent, and it was during one of these breaks that we saw a strange thing. Coming down the very steep fellside up to our right was a lone hiker. He was completely off-piste and we assumed he was taking a short cut down from Fairfield to join the path we were on. We had climbed above him before he reached our path, and we were surprised, a little later, to see that he had continued in a straight line down the steep bank to the stream, and was climbing up the even steeper bank on the other side. He was still not on any recognised path. We concluded that he was either a masochist or very lost. He may still be up there.

We eventually made it to the tarn, and circled round it.

A.Wainwright suggested two options of high level routes from here. One way went over St. Sunday Crag, and the other went over Helvellyn. So it was a choice between more climbing, much more climbing, or going straight ahead over the pass and down the valley. After considering the options for almost five seconds we decided to go straight ahead down Grisedale (surprised, aren't you?) It was very windy, and we wandered about looking for a sheltered spot to have a break in, but they had all been taken by

Almost at Grisedale tarn.
Eric at low ebb!

Day 5: Grasmere to Patterdale

earlier birds. In our search, we came across the lone walker and Alsatian again; he admitted that he'd found the climb quite tough too, which made us feel better. There followed a pleasant descent, enhanced by a rainbow, down to Patterdale; where we found our B & B immediately. Grisedale Lodge was a well appointed house, very well run by Mrs Barker-Martin.

Later, we walked along to the White Lion to eat and overindulged a bit, treating ourselves to a whisky. There was still no signal on that damned phone; it was showing a symbol telling us there was a message for us but it wouldn't divulge it. Fortunately a phone box by the pub stepped in as understudy, and after using it to book in at Bampton Grange for the following night, we stumbled back in pitch darkness.

Approaching Patterdale

DAY 6: PATTERDALE TO BAMPTON GRANGE

We breakfasted early at 8.00 a.m. as we had a long walk ahead of us. It was raining.
The prescribed route for the day was to go over the High Street range to Haweswater, then along the western bank of the reservoir. I had already had some apprehension about the route as I'm not too familiar with the area, although I did know it could be, well, navigationally challenging. It was also the highest point on A.W.'s route.

The poor weather gave us a good excuse to opt for the chickens' route again. Even A.W. recommended not going over High Street if the weather was bad. He suggested walking along the east side of Ullswater through Howtown and onwards all the way to Pooley Bridge, then crossing Askham Fell on a well hoofed bridle-path to Bampton. I am surprised that A.W. did not spot the useful bridle-path which goes from Howtown up to Askham Fell, thus avoiding Pooley Bridge and reducing the trek by about one and a half miles. Anyway, that was the way we went. With l5 miles to go, we left Patterdale at 9.00 a.m. It was still raining with that dogged Lakeland persistence that makes your heart sink; as you just know it's going to last all day. One thing that lifted our spirits a bit was that we were now on the reverse side of the first Coast to Coast strip map, which meant we were roughly a quarter of the way. But on the down side, it had taken us five days to get this far and, unless we stepped up the pace, the walk was going to take us three weeks.
We had walked the lakeside path to Howtown before, so we knew we were missing some lovely views, as the cloud level was at about, ...er, ground level. No problems navigating, of course, just keep the lake on the left and don't fall in. After a few miles we came across a barn and lurked just inside it for a while. It was very smelly and uncomfortable, so it wasn't too much hardship to carry on in the rain. We were plodding along, and I was just thinking that I hadn't had so much fun since I last cleaned the cooker, when we saw our first other walkers. A couple were coming towards us. I greeted them with the words "Aha, more mad humans!" There was a brief pause before the lady replied "Oh - mad humans - Yes."
They were Dutch, and had walked from Pooley Bridge. Their English was excellent and we chatted for a while about the eccentricities of the human race that made people walk for miles in the rain for fun.

Day 6: Patterdale to Bampton Grange

The Dutch gentleman tried to convince us that being wet was really just a state of mind. He failed.
We approached Howtown with the comforting knowledge that amongst its three or four buildings was The Howtown hotel, complete with public bar.
We squelched in and spread our soggies around the bar to drip on the flagged floor. This wasn't as anti- social as it sounds, since we were the only customers - can't imagine why!
We had some tea and scones which we made last as long as possible......but it was still raining.
We left Howtown in a steady downpour and climbed wearily up the bridle-path.

It was wet underfoot and got wetter as we got higher. One of the landmarks I was looking for was a junction of paths at a ford. This proved to be quite tricky, as the whole area was now one big ford and there seemed to be paths all over the place. Happily I chose the right one and in the fullness of time we crossed the river bridge into Bampton Grange. The river was gleefully spreading itself across the surrounding fields and ducks were swimming around where sheep should have been. We were booked in at one of the two village pubs, the Crown and Mitre.

The landlady, Wendy Frith, was very helpful in drying us out and soon most of our belongings were steaming in the airing cupboard. The pub was quite big, and strangely quiet, there were many guest rooms, but we were the only ones staying there. We ate at the pub and were rather puzzled at the total lack of customers considering it was a Friday. Wendy told us that the other pub was closing down and was having a "drinking up" weekend to get rid of all the stock. Damn! we'd picked the wrong pub!
It would have been unseemly to rush up the road for a half-price pint, so we kept Wendy company. We went to bed to the sound of Bampton Grange Church clock which must have been having lessons from Eric Morecambe; it played all the wrong notes!

Phone was still sulking - no signal.

DAY 7: BAMPTON GRANGE TO ORTON

We retrieved our clothes from the airing cupboard and breakfasted in chilly isolation in a large dining room. It had an unusual feature in the form of a dumb waiter, don't see many of them these days!

We left Bampton Grange at an un- noticed time, but we did notice it was raining. The way led pleasantly through fields of cows and curious calves to Shap Abbey. Shap Abbey warranted a photograph but didn't tempt us to explore it. In the lanes around the abbey we kept coming across a cheery postlady in her red van (Postwoman Pat?)

One mile of showers later we entered the northern end of Shap. We had coffee and the obligatory sticky bun in a small cafe, then walked the length of Shap to our exit route at the southern end. Judging by what we saw on our brief passage through, Shap has little to commend it.

Shap Abbey, almost hidden among the trees

Day 7: Bampton Grange to Orton

We called in a newsagent to restock our chocolate mine, and when we came out the rain was coming down in stair-rods. The newsagent's window suddenly became extremely interesting and we lurked under the shop awning while we studied it in detail...............It still rained!

The newsagent popped his head out and helpfully told us that this was completely normal weather for Shap and was quite likely to last until March. We realised that we couldn't wait that long, and paddled off eastwards. Quite soon we were crossing the footbridge over the M6. What an experience that was! The bridge felt very exposed and, with a strong wind blowing, rain falling, and traffic roaring underneath, it etched itself on my mind, filed under "Activities not to be repeated." The mile or so after the motorway wasn't too pretty either, as the route crossed a quarry site, with all its accompanying mess; but after passing a small hamlet called Oddendale the scenery improved. The weather on the other hand hadn't improved much and we took shelter under some trees at Potrigg. Whilst there we met a lady, a professional dog walker, who was struggling to get her hood up whilst holding eight dog leads. I relieved her of a handful of dogs whilst she sorted herself out and she disappeared into the rain; octet of dogs in tow.

We followed shortly after (although we didn't see her again; she seemed to vanish into thin air) and soon we came across a puzzling signpost. I had been following our progress on the map closely and I was expecting the path to bear left. Therefore I couldn't understand why we found a signpost like this.
This suggested to me that we should go right. We decided to ignore it and a little further on we came across another one. The penny dropped then, we were supposed to follow the posts, not the arrows!

    Must have sent an Irish chap out to mark the route (apologies to our Irish friends).
From there we had no problems; by that time it was fairly dry overhead, and not bad underfoot. We saw some peculiar snails with a black and white spiral pattern. Since returning home I have looked for them in my available books but I haven't identified them. It was a good day for birds too, we saw several

Day 7: Bampton Grange to Orton

buzzards on the moor, and as we approached Orton we got quite a close sighting of one in some trees. We also saw a few herons. We arrived at Orton where we were booked in at The George. Orton is a very pretty village, spacious and well tended, with attractive grey stone cottages, and an orderly stream flowing through the centre.

The mobile phone was actually working! I managed to get the messages from it. They were both from my brothers, each wishing us well and asking for a progress report. We made hay while the sun shone, and rang round family and friends to brag a bit, as we were feeling smug at having got through the Lakes.
That evening we ate in The George, chilli-con-carne and Black Sheep beer. What more can you ask?

There was an additional treat for Eric when two teenage girls in micro-skirts came in to play pool.
Thought I'd never get him out of the bar!

Crossing the M6 earlier in the day marked roughly one third of the walk, but since this happened on day seven we were still looking at three weeks for the total distance. Perhaps we wouldn't get into the Guinness Book of Records after all!

DAY 8: ORTON TO KIRKBY STEPHEN

By now, we had established a fairly slick routine. Early breakfast, pack up, pay bill, hit the road. At the other end of the day, we'd check in, and then whenever possible do our (my) daily chore of washing socks and undies. On a couple of occasions the B&B ladies did washing for us, but mostly I did it and dried things on radiators. I was keeping a daily diary, and also swotting up on the route ahead, and selecting accommodation.

The other unmissable activity of the day was a bath. This was essential in our opinion, not so much for hygiene as for its therapeutic value. During a long hike, especially in inclement weather, the prospect of the long hot soak at the end of it kept us going.

The morning of day eight was beautiful, just the kind of thing we'd envisaged when we chose October for the walk. There had been a heavy frost which was crunchily evident on the grass and fallen autumn leaves. We left Orton at 9.20 a.m. under a clear blue sky and a bright sun. We walked initially along quiet lanes and then through fields of grazing cattle, all the while with distant views of the Howgills to the south.

On the lonely road east of Sunbiggin Tarn, looking south towards the Howgills.

Day 8: Orton to Kirkby Stephen

After crossing a stretch of moorland approaching Sunbiggin Tarn, we walked for about one and a half miles along a lonely road. Road walking, although it is quicker, always seems longer, and it was a long long one and a half miles before we reached the landmark of the second cattle grid. Here we turned left into a soggy moorland pasture. We had a rest break at some erratics just before the site of Severals Settlement. A.W. was right when he said there was little to see at Severals. Perhaps it's more apparent from the air, but we certainly wouldn't have known it was a site of historical interest.

As we descended towards Smardale Bridge we were surprised to hear motor bikes, and saw a large group of trail bikers coming down off Smardale Fell. They crossed the bridge and disappeared westwards along the green lane.

We couldn't thumb a lift as they were going the wrong way.

On Smardale Moor we stopped to watch some sheep. Two of the sheep, which I think were ewes, not rams, were squaring up to each other and occasionally butting heads. The other sheep were clustered round, apparently egging on the fighters. Then, in the manner of human brawls on the

Lunch break near the invisible site of Severals

THE ROUTE

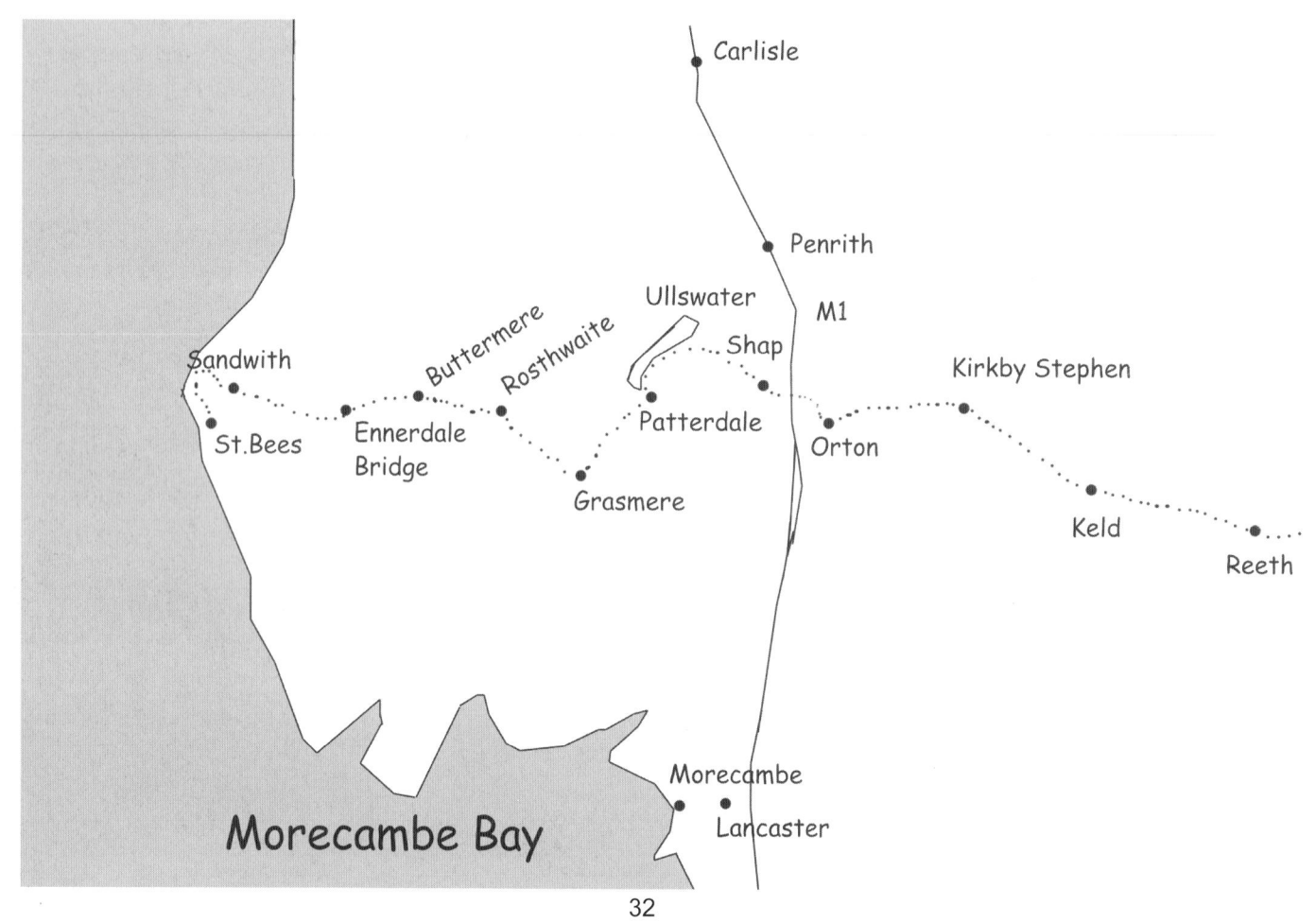

THE ROUTE

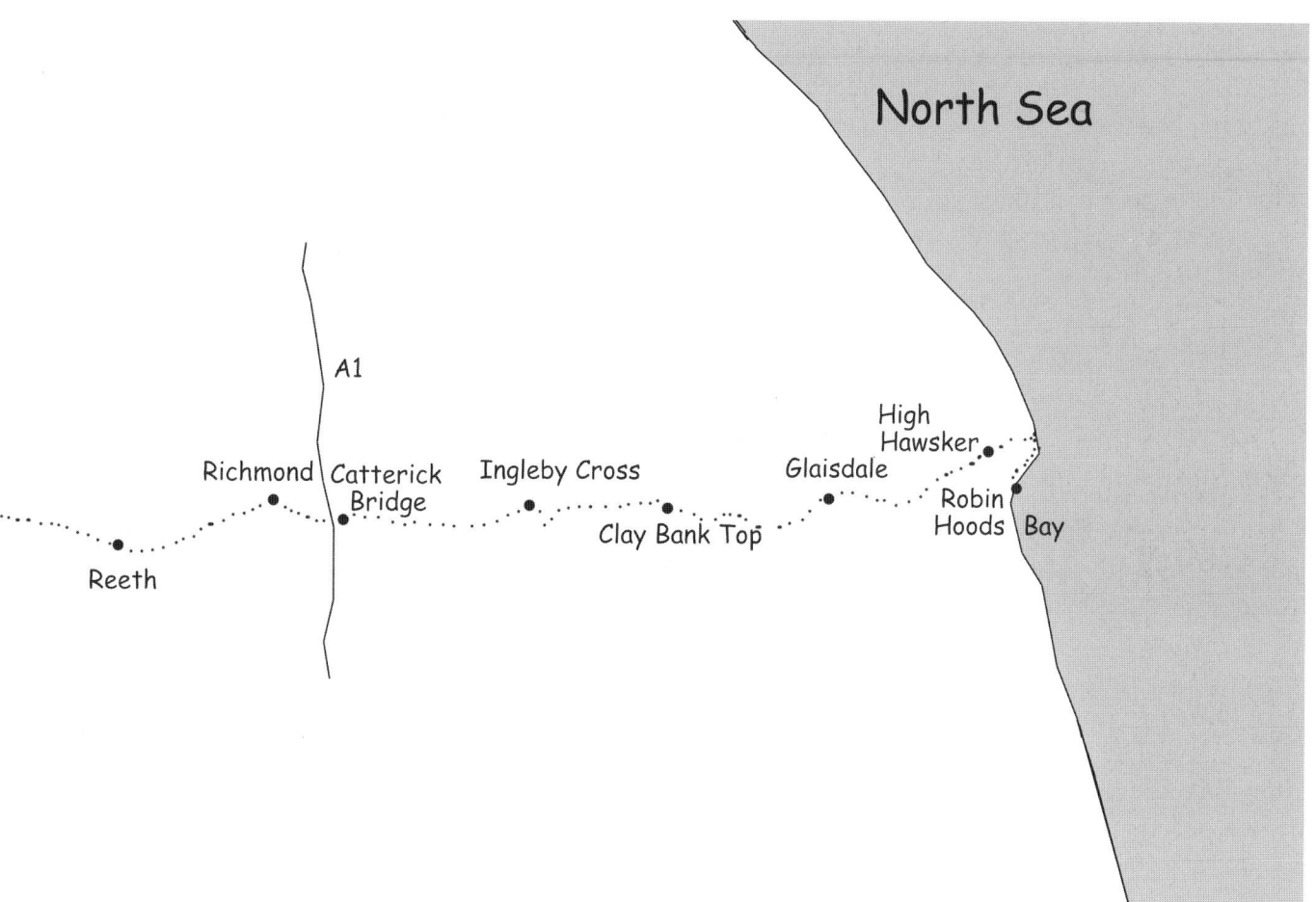

Day 8: Orton to Kirkby Stephen

football field, the onlookers all joined in, and for about thirty seconds it was an unseemly free-for-all. At some unseen signal, they all stopped and resumed grazing! We couldn't decide who to book, so we left them to it.

The remainder of the route to Kirkby Stephen was easy going, and familiar. We had walked this bit once before whilst staying at Ravenstonedale, although we'd walked in the opposite direction then.

On the approach to Kirkby Stephen we made an effort to clean our boots up as they were horribly muddy. We had booked in at one of the High Street pubs, and the landlady had agreed to leave the front door open for us, as we expected to arrive during non-opening hours. The door was unlocked, as promised, but it was one of those odd entrances consisting of two doors, each about two feet wide, designed to be opened simultaneously. However, only one door was unlocked, and we couldn't get through with our rucksacks on. We got in eventually and found ourselves in a small entrance hall where there was barely room for two people, let alone two with rucksacks. After ringing a bell in the hall, we were admitted to the bar by a bar-lady straight from central casting, a bustling brassy blonde in her sixties.

As she showed us up to our room, she said that should we want to go out before opening up time of 7.00 p.m. we should use the back door, taking the key with us and locking up as we went. The room we were allocated was buried under a quarter of an inch of dust. It was also dingy, cold, threadbare and corridor-like, but apart from that it was just fine.

We attempted to perform our daily routine. The bath bit was OK, since neither of us are arachnophobes, so we weren't troubled by the tarantulas on the ceiling. The laundry, however, was a non-starter, as you can't dry washing in a fridge.

We were unanimous that we didn't fancy eating in the pub we were in, so at 6.30p.m. we went downstairs to try to find the back door. I opened a door and found

Day 8: Orton to Kirkby Stephen

a long dark corridor. "Have you found anything?" enquired Eric.
"Yes, a notice which says Beware of the Dog."
"Oh, can you see anything further in?"
"Er.......a very large dog bed."
We crept on nervously and found another door with a key in it. I opened it half expecting a mastiff to leap out, but it led to a side yard and freedom.
We dined at a different pub, which from the outside looked better than ours, but the place had delusions of grandeur and the food was disappointing. Whilst we were alone in the dining room eating our measly meal, a couple came into the pub who had the exhausted air of long-distance walkers. A bit of eavesdropping confirmed that they too were Coast-to-Coasters. They had walked that day from Shap, which should have been 22 miles, but had taken a wrong turn which extended the walk to 25 miles. They had still been in the countryside when it became too dark to map read. They had no torch, and the girl was wearing trainers. It made us feel quite competent!
We returned to the dingy pub. We decided to have a last drink before going to bed, and went to the bar where the landlady was trying to get a domino game going. We didn't move out of the way fast enough and found ourselves drawn into a game with the landlady, the milkman and the chip shop man. Two minutes into the game, the landlady mentioned that the rules were that the loser bought the round.

We played two games. I lost one, Eric lost the other. Strange, that!

We managed to detach ourselves and went up to bed before bankruptcy set in. We didn't have such a good night as our corridor was at the front of the pub and heavy traffic was trundling past our window from dusk till dawn; then the rush hour started. One cause for celebration raised its head when we realised that we had enjoyed our second completely dry day, perhaps as well, considering the total lack of comfort and drying facilities!

DAY 9: KIRKBY STEPHEN TO KELD

We rose, and made our way to the dining room, carefully avoiding the hole in the floor boards on the landing, which was cunningly covered in carpet. After breakfast we were followed back to our room by a cat who explored the dust under the bed while we packed.

When we were ready to leave, we dusted the cat and asked our hostess whether she preferred a cheque or a Switch card, and she helpfully told us where the nearest cash machine was. We took the hint and got some cash, which doubtless went straight into the pinny pocket.

We left Kirkby Stephen at 9.35 a.m. to do 12 miles to Keld. The first few miles were easy to follow, but the climb out of Kirkby Stephen was very steep. There was a huge amount of aerial activity, low flying fighter planes playing war games and shattering the peace.

As we climbed up towards increasingly bleak moorland it started to rain. I decided to change from breeches to

The long climb out of Kirkby Stephen.

Day 9: Kirkby Stephen to Keld

waterproof trousers. This was quite tricky, involving the removal of bumbag, rucksack, gaiters and boots in order to get the breeches off, then hopping around in undies whilst trying to get everything back on again. When I'd done I found I was standing on my breeches so they had a soggy boot print on them. Naturally it had also stopped raining by then.

Shortly after, we found a large notice which explained that because the moor was suffering from erosion, walkers were requested to follow different routes across it at different times of the year. We had to follow the blue route. The notice, whilst very informative, omitted to say "Impassable bogs ahead", or "Abandon hope all ye who enter here," which would have given us some idea of the condition of the blue route.

From there on, the "path" varied between being horrendous to totally impassable. It took us an eternity to find a way to the Nine Standards without drowning. When we finally got there they weren't worth the effort. We naively thought that from there it would get better, as we were on the summit, and water flows downhill.

But no one has educated the water on Nine Standards Rigg, it clung to the moor top like a shipwrecked sailor to a life raft. The moor was criss-crossed with a pattern of groughs. A grough is a sort of gully. The sides of the gully, usually about six or eight feet deep, are near vertical and formed of soggy spongy peat. The bottom, anything from 5 ft. to 20 ft. across, is liquid slime of unknown depth. Sometimes a grough stretches from horizon to horizon. We spent most of the next hour trying to cross groughs. When we weren't in groughs we were in bogs.

In one of the bogs Eric was caught unawares and sank up to his knee. After a major struggle he extracted his leg and I was quite relieved to see that both his foot and his boot were still on the end of it.

We weren't much impressed by Nine Standards Rigg. It went on for miles.........and miles.

Ahead of us we could see a group of four walkers who seemed to be struggling even more than we were. They must have been, as we were steadily gaining on them. We eventually caught them up and found that they were

Day 9: Kirkby Stephen to Keld

Coast to Coasters too. We briefly compared notes as to what we would have said and done to A.Wainwright had he been accessible just at that moment, and then we overtook them and slithered on.

Memory would deem that the moor stretched for about 6 miles. The map suggests only 4 miles, but of course that doesn't allow for all the deviations; trying to find ways round glutinous goo.

I think Eric and I are pretty confident that we shall not be going that way again.

At the end of the moorland marathon, near a farm called Ravenseat, we came across a B road and decided to

Nine Standards looking deceptively close

Day 9: Kirkby Stephen to Keld

abandon the prescribed route in favour of its dry tarmac surface. We followed it for half a mile, then branched left on a footpath which led us to the B road to Keld. The footpath took us through a field containing a bull, but fortunately he didn't notice us.

The day brightened considerably when we arrived at Betty and David Cox's house in Keld. David let us in to a small hall where we removed our boots and put them with some other boots and a pair of muddy trainers which were already there. In the kitchen we found the owners of the boots and trainers; the couple we had seen the previous evening who had been lost en route to Kirkby Stephen.

They were Ann and Francisco, Californians from Sacramento. They had come to England specifically to do the

Keld

Day 9: Kirkby Stephen to Keld

walk, having seen details of it on the Internet. They had made the enviable decision not to cross Nine Standards Rigg, and had come to Keld from Kirkby Stephen by road. Consequently they not only had dry feet, but also had had the benefit of Betty's warm kitchen, tea and scones for one hour longer than us.

The atmosphere in the large country kitchen was lovely and the six of us chatted happily whilst Betty baked. Later, when we had removed all the peat from our persons, Ann, Francisco, Eric and I tried valiantly to eat a meal which would have fed eight of us quite adequately. Ann and Francisco must have experienced quite a dramatic change when they came to England for the walk. During the summer in Sacramento they had had over thirty consecutive days at over $100^{o}C$, and had then flown to England to cold, rain and peat bogs.

And we thought we were mad!

The four of us congratulated each other on having reached Keld. However, just as we were getting cramp from patting ourselves on the back, Betty told us about one guest who had stayed with her who was registered blind, and was doing the walk alone.

Clever bugger!

Right: Low Bridge near Keld

DAY 10: KELD TO REETH

Keld is half way! This meant that we had accelerated a bit and were now on course for an eighteen day finish. It also meant we could start on Map No.2 - Keld to Robin Hood's Bay, all downhill from here - metaphorically speaking.

The morning was bright and frosty. We were surprised to find the breakfast table set for six people, but the mystery was solved when a couple came in from the house next door, which was usually a holiday let.
After the previous day's experience we had grave doubts about following another of A.W.'s "high" routes, but the good weather tempted us to have a go at it. This proved to be the right decision as the paths turned out to be firm and dry, and we made good progress.

The valley floor of Swaledale was covered in a hard frost, which was lovely to look at. The waterfalls, Kisdon Force and East Gill Force were flowing fast and furiously. We climbed up past Crackpot Hall, where there was some evidence of renovation, or perhaps just preservation, to Swinner Gill. A couple of years ago, with some friends in tow, we wasted a lot of time and effort searching Swinner Gill for a "hidden" cave, which was once used as a place of worship, and is reputed to be up there. It must be very well hidden because we couldn't find it, and Eric and I didn't spend any more time looking for it on this visit.

From Swinner Gill the path climbed up through mining wastelands to Gunnerside Moor. At Gunnerside Gill a lone worker was doing "make safe" building work on the ruinous mine buildings. From there, another short climb took us to Melbecks Moor. We looked back and could see a group of four about a mile behind us, still on Gunnerside Moor. It was the group we had met on Nine Standards Rigg.

Melbecks Moor also displayed extensive mining scars, but we could look past it all to distant hills. We dropped down to Old Gang beck and followed it down a long long valley on a good track to reach Swaledale again at

Day 10: Keld to Reeth

Healaugh. If we had been dedicated A.W. followers we wouldn't have been at Healaugh, but we had got on the low path rather than the high one at Surrender Bridge. No matter.
The day spoiled itself one and a half miles from Reeth by raining. When we reached Reeth we fancied some tea and a bun, and went in the first cafe we came across, which was accessed through a bread shop. Our arrival won us some black looks from the proprietor, who had furnished his cafe with a nice light grey carpet. One has to question the wisdom of this in a Dales village which must teem with walkers all year round, but there you go.

We stubbornly had our tea and bun, and on the way out belatedly noticed a sign on the door saying "No boots." Since the only options available would have been either to leave them cluttering up the bread shop, or outside in the rain, I didn't think it was a very practical request, if indeed, it was a "request" at all, as I can't remember seeing the word "Please" anywhere.
Perhaps what was really meant was "No hikers."

Right: Frost in Swaledale from Crackpot Hall.

Day 10: Keld to Reeth

We went on to find our B&B, a lady called Jennifer Davies, who had been recommended to us by Mr & Mrs. Cox. Jennifer was a tall forthright lady who had the confident air of a public school headmistress. She had two Border collies who were mother and daughter but didn't get on at all. Conversations with Jennifer were punctuated by growls and tussles at floor level as the dogs argued and jostled for attention.

We were plied with tea and biccies (needn't have troubled the unwelcoming cafe owner had we known) and then went through our usual daily bath and laundry rituals. That evening we ate at The Buck, where we met the four Nine Standards Rigg walkers and found out a little more about them. They were Dennis and Lyn from Wales, and John and Judith from Buxton. From then on, between ourselves, we always referred to them as The Welsh Team.

The food, beer and company were all most agreeable and we had a fine evening.

106 miles down, only 84 to go.

Right: The old mine buildings at Gunnerside Gill.

DAY 11: REETH TO BROMPTON ON SWALE

The morning found us in the company of a rather strange pair of Germans and a lot of water. The Germans were at the breakfast table and the water was falling from the sky outside. The Germans were both male. One was very thin, and the other was about 25 stones. The thin one spoke quite good English, which was fortunate for the sake of mutual conversation, since neither Eric nor I speak German. They were from Cologne, and were on holiday. The breakfast was excellent, with fresh fruit salad and yoghurt on offer besides all the usual breakfasty things.

It was still showery when we left Reeth at 9.10 a.m. and was also very windy. The recommended day's mileage was only ten and a half miles to Richmond. As the following day's was 23 miles, we had decided to extend the walk to fifteen miles, which would take us to Brompton-on-Swale. After a couple of miles the path climbed up through a wood. I could hear what sounded like a chainsaw and kept expecting to come across a lumberjack, but, rather alarmingly, the noise turned out to be two tree trunks rubbing together violently in the wind. We rushed past half expecting them to fall around our ears, but made it without mishap.

From thereon we went through numerous fields divided by stone walls with squeeze stiles in them. These stiles were not designed for either hiking boots or rucksacks. There is only room for one boot, and you have to sort of shuffle forwards with one boot in line behind the other, like a sand dancer.

We passed an interesting house called 'Ellers.' It had no access road and was a half mile from the nearest B road.

The walk into Richmond was uneventful, though quite muddy underfoot. As we were entering the town Ann and Francisco caught us up. They were making Richmond their overnight stop. It was still early afternoon, so they had a half day to explore the town.

However, we still had five miles to go, and we decided we wanted some food before going on. We failed to find a cafe displaying a sign reading "Disgustingly muddy walkers welcome," so we bought drinks and sandwiches and picnicked in the square.

Day 11: Reeth to Brompton on Swale

When we were ready to go I found that some 'orrible bird had messed on my rucksack. This is supposed by some to be a lucky sign, but the only lucky aspect I could see about it was that it had missed me and, more importantly, my sandwich. Rucksack cleaned up, we set off to do the five miles to Brompton-on-Swale. We could have walked the whole way on B roads, but the A.W. route, following the Swale, looked quite attractive on paper, which just goes to show what a lying toad paper can be. Initially there were no problems, although the paths, like almost all the ones we'd been on before, were very muddy. We met an elderly gentleman going the opposite way who warned us of a fallen signpost near Hagg Farm, and said he'd missed his way there. When we reached Hagg Farm, or the site of it, since it no longer exists, we tried hard to follow the map through the ensuing fields. However, we climbed over one stile to find ourselves in one of those huge, ghastly ploughed fields that seem to stretch for miles. The signpost was laid dead in the ditch, so no clues there. We trudged across in what I thought was the right direction, but on arrival at the far side, with 2 lb. of mud stuck to each boot, we found a locked gate.

Richmond in the mist

Day 11: Reeth to Brompton on Swale

Now we know from sad experience that a locked gate doesn't necessarily mean you're on the wrong track, and beyond the gate we could see that the track led to a ford, which tied in with our map and instructions. So, over the gate we went, and then through the ford, which was rather too deep for comfort but cleaned our boots up, and thus arrived at another locked gate. Eric climbed it first, and briefly he laid along the top of it with a leg and an arm on either side, a picture of dejection.

The gate led to a lane which soon took us to the small village of Colburn, which was where we wanted to be, although we did seem to arrive in the village from the wrong direction. We left Colburn on a bridle path which, according to A.W., "runs pleasantly east with the Swale on the left." This is obviously a misprint, and should read "runs swampily east, with the contents of the Swale all around." That bridle path should have had a government health warning on it. It gave me visions of horses with trench - hoof. Whilst I was wading across the morass, there was mutiny in the ranks. My right leg went on strike and seized up at the hip. It had done 122 miles and it thought that that was enough. I refused to give in to its pleas to be put in a taxi and sent home, and my left leg and I dragged it along, complaining all the way.

Things got worse when we reached the A1. Up till then the path had been about 30 ft. above river level (in theory) but it slithered down a muddy bank to go underneath the road. Eric went before me, and I was carefully picking my way, watching where I was putting my feet, when I glanced down just in time to see Eric rolling down the hill to land rucksack - first in the mire at the bottom.

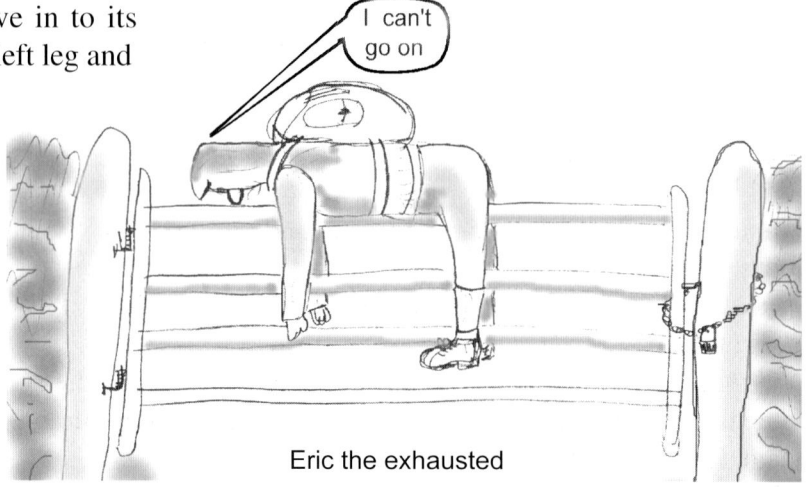

Eric the exhausted

Day 11: Reeth to Brompton on Swale

He was OK, but absolutely plastered with mud; hands, body, rucksack, everything! Very anti-social. It was futile trying to clean him up there so we carried on and I dropped back a bit, hoping that people wouldn't realise we were together. We soon reached Catterick Bridge.

We were booked in at a Hotel at Brompton-on-Swale .... yes, a Hotel, not a B & B, but we didn't know exactly where it was. We discussed whether to phone them for directions, but then spotted a sign to Brompton-on-Swale and decided to follow it. Brompton didn't look that big on the map so we expected to find the hotel easily. It was only a half a mile to the village, but seemed further as we were getting tired and grumpy (as opposed to the "tired but happy" state of most jolly walkers I seem to read about).

We reached the village centre without finding the hotel, and I decided to ask directions at the pub. As I crossed over the road towards the pub door the publican came running out to meet me. He'd probably seen the state we were in and was trying to keep his carpet clean. "Are you looking for the camping barn luv?" We clearly looked even worse than I'd thought. He gave us directions to the hotel, and guess what? the bloody place was back at Catterick Bridge where we'd just come from! The next time I'm considering phoning for directions I'll do it.

We trudged back the half mile, then up past the sewage works, and then we found it. The hotel's name, we decided, had given us a false impression of what to expect. It was a roadhouse. But never mind, the lady there was welcoming and brought out (at our request) a bucket of hot soapy water to enable Eric to get the worst of the grime off outside. We were then taken through the bar, where there was a free-flying grey parrot, and upstairs to the biggest hotel room I've ever been in.

The room contained two double beds, one single bed and a large amount of heavy old bedroom furniture, and it was still spacious. On the downside, it was extremely dingy, and looked as though Victoria could have been on the throne when it was last decorated. My spirits rose when I saw that it had ensuite facilities, and sank again when I peeked in and saw the shower. Our first ensuite room and we were deprived of an hour long soak in the bath. Life can be cruel.

Day 11: Reeth to Brompton on Swale

We discovered that we had a rare signal on the mobile phone and decided that we'd better take advantage of it and book the remainder of our accommodation. We thought this was a particularly cunning move in view of the fact that we seemed to be meeting more people on the walk, and we also knew that the school half-term holiday was coming up. B & B's on the North York Moors section of the walk, the final stretch, seemed not only to be thin on the ground, but also on ground rather further from the route than was desirable. Although there was a vague hint in the accommodation guide that transport might be available to some of the more distant ones, it wasn't clear how this might happen. We had a period of mild panic when the first few places I called were either full, closed or out. But after a determined effort I managed to book us in to the end of the trip. Two of the bookings I made were at places well off - piste, and pick - up arrangements had to be agreed upon. I came off the phone feeling very harassed and with my trusty little accommodation guide covered in scribbled notes, I just hoped I hadn't left any holes anywhere, or booked us in at two places on the same night. I needed a drink! We went down to the bar. The parrot wouldn't talk to us so we made friends with Elvis the cat instead. In the bar we met John, Judith, Dennis and Lyn, who were also staying at the hotel. We compared our day over a drink or two and a bar meal. They already knew about Eric's close encounter of the swampy kind. News, especially that of others misfortune, travels fast. They were all clean and smug, having walked from Richmond to Catterick Bridge by road. It appeared we had picked the wrong route for the day yet again.

We went upstairs at our usual early hour, and after an evening stroll round the bedroom, we went to bed, but were woken by a most horrendous noise outside and violent tremors through the building, as what sounded like a column of Sherman tanks passed outside our window at great speed. I thougmust be morning but it was 3.50 a.m. We got up and put our earplugs in, whilst muttering uncomplimentary things about the army. At 6.45 a.m. a damned radio alarm in the room went off, and, without my glasses, I spent ages trying to find the right knobs to shut the bloody thing up. In the end I just turned the volume down as far as possible and left the problem to someone else. All in all it was not a good night.

DAY 12: BROMPTON ON SWALE TO INGLEBY CROSS

Or, as in our case, Catterick Bridge to Ingleby Cross. We went blearily down to breakfast with the knowledge that we had the longest day's walk to date ahead of us, seventeen and a half miles. We left the hotel with no regrets at 8.50 a.m. We knew that a fair proportion of the day's walk was on roads and lanes, and after the previous day's experience we weren't sorry either.

The walking was easy, if a little dreary, and we didn't see much of interest en route except a magnificent treehouse at Streetlam, which warranted a photograph. We called at the White Swan at Danby Whiske. Contrary to the experience of A.W. this is now a thriving pub, taking full advantage of its position on the route. We had some tasty soup, and were soon joined by the Welsh team.

The landlord had started a practice of asking Coast-to-Coasters to sign a book, and we duly obliged. Dennis kept us amused by looking through it and reading out some of the humorous comments, like "Going well, going mad, going home." In the afternoon Ingleby Cross was a long time coming. The terrain was flat and navigation straightforward, but it was a rather dull walk. Eric and I were the first to arrive. We were booked in at the Blue Bell Inn, where the Welsh team were also staying.

Splendid tree house at Streetlam

Day 12: Brompton on Swale to Ingleby Cross

The Blue Bell was closed when we arrived, but there was a blackboard outside which told us which room we were in. The accommodation was in a purpose built block behind the pub.

At the Blue Bell they had clearly done a survey to determine the minimum requirements of the average Coast-to-Coaster. The result was a row of cells, each containing two single beds, a radiator, a coat tree and a chair, with an en suite shower and loo. We were in Cell 2. It was perfectly adequate but it was disappointing to have a shower again after a seventeen and a half mile walk. It was even more disappointing when I went in the beast and found that the shower head was so clogged up you had to run around to get wet.

We ate in the pub which had an abundance of horse racing pictures. The barman was a smallish man who seemed to have an old back injury, we wondered if he'd been a jockey. The Welsh team were in the bar, as were the local darts team, having a pre-match practice. We expected Ann and Francisco (the American team) to turn up too, as the barman thought they were staying nearby. They had tried to book at the Blue Bell but had been too late to get a room. They didn't appear at the pub, and we later found out that they had had to go to Osmotherley; a mile or two down the road. We must have made our telephone bid for accommodation just in time.

We retired to our cell at 10.00 p.m. We had a bit of first aid to attend to as we had both developed a mysterious rash on our legs where the rib of our socks had been rubbing.

Long Distance Leg Lurgy!

Iris and Brian, brief walking companions on Carlton Moor

DAY 13: INGLEBY CROSS TO CLAY BANK TOP

Before setting out we spent considerable time putting cream on our legs and deliberating over clothing. We finally decided that fresh air might be the solution, so packed gaiters away and put on shorts. We really felt to be making progress now, as we were on the final quarter of the strip map. So, we left Ingleby Cross at 9.00 a.m., striding briskly passed the biggest rat I have ever seen laid dead, fortunately, in the gutter. The path soon plunged into a silent fir forest and led gently upwards to join the Cleveland Way, and emerged by a TV relay station on the hilltop. We were to follow the Cleveland Way for the rest of the day, which improved our walking conditions no end. Thanks to some sterling work done by the North York Moors National Park, the paths were in Al condition.

The day's walk was a splendid one, one of the best we had. It involved nearly 2700 feet of up and 2180 feet of down, spread over five ascents and descents and twelve miles. The weather was wonderful, it was an ideal temperature, no wind, and we had clear views.

Looking back across the Vale of Mowbray

Day 13: Ingleby Cross to Clay Bank Top

At the foot of the second ascent we met Brian and Iris, a couple who were out for a day's walk to the Lordstones Cafe and back. We walked with them for two or three miles, pausing for photos at the cairn on top of Carlton bank. Shortly after, we arrived at the cafe, which is built underground, in a disused alum mine I think. We lunched there with Brian and Iris, who then set off on the return journey. We had been caught up at the cafe by the Welsh and American teams, and after lunch we had a Coast-to-Coasters team photo taken outside, before tackling the last four or five miles together. Almost as soon as we had set off, John fell and made an admirable attempt at Eric's mud-covering record set on day eleven. He didn't really come close, but the effect was very impressive as he was wearing a cream Arran sweater. I walked most of the way with Lyn, and in addition to covering the miles, we also covered a variety of topics, from Meindl boots to Mums-in-Law. Along the way we were

The Coast to Coasters at Lordstones Cafe

Standing left to right: Eric, Lyn, Anne, Francisco, Dennis and John.

Kneeling: the author and Judith

Day 13: Ingleby Cross to Clay Bank Top

treated to our first view of the North Sea — only forty miles away now. We paused at the Wainstones, a fascinating outcrop of jumbled rocks, and took photos whilst everyone caught up. Over the years, it has become a long running joke between Eric and I that almost every time we walk anywhere, he will look at a distant hill and say "Is that Ingleborough?" Well, he said it when we were at the Wainstones, and the hill was Ingleborough, I checked!

Resting at the Wainstones

Panorama from the Wainstones, looking east; Roseberry Topping and the sea can be seen in the distance.

Day 13: Ingleby Cross to Clay Bank Top

We were all being picked up at Clay Bank Top by our various hosts and hostesses. Eric and I, and Ann and Francisco, had agreed rendezvous times of 4.30p.m, but the Welsh team had been told they could phone their hotel when they reached Clay Bank Top. This actually proved to be quite a challenge for them as there was no phone box. Fortunately, the mobile we had carted along for 153 miles reluctantly put itself out a bit and picked up a signal, so they were able to use that instead.

We were all successfully picked up and went our separate ways. We were staying with Mr & Mrs Huntley at Great Broughton. The accommodation was excellent, as had been the case with all the small B & B's we'd used on the walk. We carried out all our washing and bathing routines in luxury and, after I had cleaned the embarrassing tide-mark off the bath, Mrs. Huntley dried our laundry for us. We ate out at the Wainstones Hotel, which had such an extensive menu we dithered for ages before deciding what to eat. Unfortunately we spoilt what had been a great day by seeing a forecast for the following day. It was gruesome!

DAY 14 : CLAY BANK TOP TO THE LION AT BLAKEY

Last night's bed was wonderfully comfortable, we made a big mistake when we left it in the morning. The A.W. recommended distance for the day was 19 miles to Glaisdale. We had decided that that was too far for comfort and were only doing 9 miles to the Lion. The bad forecast was spot on, it was gruesome from the first step. In Great Broughton it was raining fairly heavily and a bit windy. Mr. Huntley dropped us off at Clay Bank Top, where it was even windier, and we had quite a fight to get all our gear on and hatches battened down.

Bravely (I thought) we started the climb up to Greenhow Moor. Somewhere nearby there was probably a sign reading "The Nightmare Starts Here," but we missed it in the mist, or maybe we mist it in the missed. We could see only one other human, a lone walker ahead of us. When we reached the exposed moor top the full horror of the weather hit us. Visibility was about 30 yards. The rain was being driven from the south by a terrific, screaming wind which threatened to carry me off Scotlandwards. The path was well - blazed, or I would have chickened out there and then, but we struggled on. I had my head down trying to shield my face and I only just noticed a man walking in the opposite direction. It was the lone walker we had seen earlier. Obviously he'd thought "Sod this for a game of soldiers" and was off back home. Wise man. Shame he didn't invite us too.

We held hands in an attempt to anchor each other down. We hadn't gone far when Eric said:
    "I want to pee!"
    "Oh bloody hell!"
Having a pee, even for Eric, was a complicated business. He couldn't expose the necessary bits without dropping his waterproof trousers, which in turn meant either removing his rucksack, or having it held off his back by yours truly. Since there was nowhere respectable to put the rucksack down, I took the weight while the job was done, downgale of course. We staggered on. The route joined a disused railway line which, being raised up as opposed to countersunk, was even more exposed. I feared for my contact lenses.
We had hardly gone another mile before Eric announced he needed another pee.

Day 14: Clay Bank Top to the Lion at Blakey

`"You can't"
"I do"   So we went through the routine again, getting rapidly colder and wetter. On the raised railway banking I felt in real danger of being blown over the edge, and had to cling on to Eric's 13 stone for security. Either Eric was having a bad attack of nerves, or the rain was finding its way into his bladder, as he had to stop to pee four more times. I made the rather caustic comment that he might as well do it as he walked along, since he couldn't have got any wetter and it might have warmed his legs up. This remark was not favourably received. We also had to stop and duck down in a gully for me to turn the map over in its carrier, although I don't know why I bothered. One stretch of railway banking looks just like any other when you can only see for 30 yards. Mum's parting words were definitely ringing true.

We started to get a bit worried about wind-chill as our "waterproofs" were saturated. We were carrying a couple of black bin-liners and Eric had the idea of putting them inside our jackets, just down the front, to help keep the chill out. It was a challenge getting them in, but we managed it. I still wasn't concerned about the route, as it was apparent from the map that if we kept on the rail track we would eventually reach a tarmac road where, if we turned left, we would reach the Lion pub. Wainwright's instructions, on the other hand, were to branch off left across the moor after seeing the Lion on the horizon, but clearly that wasn't an option for us as we wouldn't have been able to see a pride of lions 50 yards away, never mind one, a mile away.

We then came across a path to the left signed L.W.W. for Lyke Wake Walk, and promptly fell into a mild marital dispute. As Chief Navigator, I was in favour of sticking to the rail-track like a limpet, on the grounds that when we reached the road we would know exactly where we were. As Chief Wet Frozen Person, Eric wanted to take the path, on the grounds that it might, just might, go to the pub. Now, I've done the Lyke Wake Walk, albeit twenty years ago, and I knew it didn't actually pass the pub, or at least it didn't in 1977. 1 didn't want to cut the corner off and reach the road only to find that we then didn't know whether to go left or right for the pub. In the end, after a bit of unseemly squabbling, we agreed to follow the path for a short distance, and retrace our steps if it looked like disappearing, or didn't seem to be getting anywhere. We set off on the path and three minutes

Day 14: Clay Bank Top to the Lion at Blakey

later we nearly walked into the wall of a building. It was 'The Lion,' and the nightmare was over.
NB Author's Note - Just for the record, I found out later that the L.W.W. has been diverted since I did it, so there!

    The entrance porch of The Lion was littered with dripping waterproofs. We added ours to the heap and dripped into the bar, which was quite full of an unusually mixed gathering. Soggy frozen hikers rubbed shoulders with the well dressed members of a wedding party. Amongst the former were Ann and Francisco, who must have been only a few hundred yards ahead of us in the murk. I went to the 'Ladies' to get some dry clothes on. This proved to be frustratingly difficult, as my hands were so cold, despite having had gloves on, that my fingers wouldn't function. It took ages even to open my rucksack, and buttons and zips proved even more taxing. The air was as blue as I was before I eventually got a dry T shirt, shorts and socks on.
    Back in the bar, I found Eric, who had changed in the 'Gents,' and we ordered a Yorkshire Pud each to warm us up. We were talking to Ann and Francisco when the door opened and the Welsh Team staggered in. We had all been tramping across the moor within a mile of each other without knowing it. Boy, were we glad that 'The Lion' was the end of the road for us that day. The others were all booked in at Glaisdale, so had another 9 miles to face. Ann, Francisco, Lyn and Judith wanted to get a taxi the rest of the way, and tried to phone for one, but no one would come. It left them with no option but to carry on. I called our B&B. We were booked with Jack and Mary Lowson at Danby Dale. Jack said he would come for us and, while we were waiting, I tried to dry our map and my money, mopping the water up with tissues. The others all heroically got ready and set out again, Captain Oates-like. When Jack arrived he proved to be an impressive figure. He had said to look out for a tall guy with white hair, and indeed he had to bend down to get in the door. He looked like a remote hill farmer with his old donkey jacket and windswept hair, and when he took us to his car it was slightly battered and contained a fair amount of straw. Considering the weather conditions he set off up the road at a worrying speed, whizzing past our Coast-to-Coast comrades who were battling through the gale. I hoped that Jack knew the road well, as he must have been driving from memory, certainly not from any visual aids. We hurtled along progressively

Day 14: Clay Bank Top to the Lion at Blakey

narrower country lanes and finally turned up a rutted grassy track. At this stage I had a premonition of ending up at a desolate hill farm with no heating and an outside loo, but I needn't have worried. Sycamore House was just as comfortable as all the other B&B's we had used. Jack gave us tea and biscuits, and dried us out. We revived ourselves in the bath and lazed away the rest of the afternoon, whilst sparing a sympathetic thought for the others, still out there. That evening Jack and Mary made a splendid meal, which was perhaps as well, as it would have been a hell of a walk to eat out anywhere.

The view from our Bed and Breakfast at Danby Dale

DAY 15: THE LION TO GLAISDALE

We awoke to discover - "The View." Danby Dale was bigger than thirty yards across after all. The sun shone, the sky was blue, all traces of mist and rain had disappeared.

After a lovely brekky, including fresh fruit salad, Mary took us back to The Lion. She talked non-stop all the way, must have been making up for the general lack of people to talk to at their isolated home. When we got out at The Lion we discovered that, although all the rest of the horrid weather had moved on, the high wind was still with us. The nine miles to Glaisdale were all on very exposed high ground, the others must have had a tough time the day before. On the route we passed a shooting box called Trough House, mentioned in A.W.'s account of the walk as "roughly furnished, and such an excellent refuge that one almost wishes it would rain cats and dogs so that advantage could be taken of its shelter."

I tried the door, and it was firmly locked. So much for the hospitality and thoughtfulness of the huntin' and shootin' brigade!   Sod the hypothermic walkers!   Let 'em die!

I can't say we enjoyed this bit of the walk. The views, though distant, weren't inspiring, and the wind was strong enough to make life uncomfortable. As we neared the end, we decided not to walk along Glaisdale Rigg, another exposed track, but instead we dropped down into Glaisdale itself to get some shelter. The walk through the dale was much more pleasant, even though it was on Tarmac. We arrived at Ashley House in Glaisdale in fairly quick time and were greeted by Mrs Cowan and tea and toasted teacakes. In our room we found a note from Dennis and Lyn, just to say they'd made it. Mrs. Cowan told us they had not arrived till 6.30 p.m. and had been so whacked they'd gone straight to bed. I'm not surprised.

We had a stroll down to look at the Railway Station, and Beggars Bridge, and picked out the footpath which was the following day's starting point.

Day 15: The Lion to Glaisdale

That evening neither of us felt hungry, but we still made the mistake of going out to the pub, just next door to our B&B. The pub was miserable, with the few occupants and barmaid glued to the soap on a telly in the corner. The food was no better, greasy and dull. There were slightly more squabbling cats and large dogs in the bar than people. We returned to Ashley House and passed a little time in the lounge. I found a book entitled something like "A Wife's Coast-to-Coast Story," and started reading through it.   **It was nauseating!**
The wife in question wrote of idyllic warm days spent basking in the sun eating delicious sandwiches provided by the previous night's B&B lady and praying, as she skipped along, to give thanks to God for such a wonderful walk.   **YUK!**

I leafed through and there wasn't a single bog or swear word in it. I cast it down in disgust as being totally unrealistic, and with dark mutterings of "wait till they read my version, they'll never go walking again," I went to bed.

Right: Beggar's Bridge at Glaisdale

DAY 16: GLAISDALE TO HIGH HAWSKER

This was our last full day of walking and the weather decided to be kind for it. On the map the route looked good, through villages and woods and along river banks. Country lanes and tracks took us past Egton Bridge to Grosmont. We spent a little time at Grosmont Station, where a steam train was puffing, and then did a little puffing ourselves up a very steep hill to Sleights Moor. The moor was easily crossed by tracks and a B road, and then we dropped down into Littlebeck, where we had our lunch stop on a convenient bench.

Above: Egton Manor Estate **Right:** Grosmont Station

Day 16: Glaisdale to High Hawsker

From there we walked up a long, long, long wooded path by May Beck. We passed The Hermitage, a shelter carved out of a large boulder, and Falling Foss, a waterfall, but I have to say that neither of them seemed worth the effort involved in getting there. The woodland path was steep, slippy, very muddy, and overstocked with treacherous tree roots. Perhaps it was just that we were starting to suffer from "Long Distance Walk Fatigue Syndrome," but we didn't appreciate the one and a half mile detour that this part of the walk entailed.

Anyway, in due course we emerged onto the B1416, which we could easily have reached from Littlebeck on nice, unmuddy, direct roads. (I didn't tell Eric.)

   The directions from there gave us a choice, either a gated road straight to Hawsker, or another deviation over another bloody moor...... No contest, the road it was. Even the road seemed to get longer as the afternoon wore on, but we arrived eventually at our final overnight stop, York House. York House was an excellent small hotel, run most efficiently by an enthusiastic young couple, Sue and Paul Newbold. The ensuite room we had was lovely, but it was a shame it had a shower and we were denied the luxury of a bath on our last night. I thought I'd be cunning and I sneaked along to a communal bathroom, but I must have been too early as the water wasn't hot! Never mind, the shower was. The hotel was licensed, and also did an evening meal, so we were able to impress the other guests with tales of our accomplishment over a pre-dinner drink. We probably didn't impress them much with our appearance as our "evening dress " was looking decidedly travel weary and crumpled by then. Sixteen days in a rucksack is not conducive to the smartness of trouser creases.

Falling Foss Waterfall

DAY 17: HIGH HAWSKER TO ROBIN HOODS BAY

It had rained heavily during the night but was fine by the time we set off at 9.30 a.m.
So we strode along the last 4 miles of cliff path. The cliffs looked remarkably similar to those at St. Bees, we could hardly spot the difference other than the amount of mud we were carrying on our boots.
It only took one and a half hours to reach Robin Hoods Bay. As we were entering the outskirts we spotted Derick strolling down to the beach, and we followed him down there; performed the photo-call in the sea and that was that.

Might do it hopping backwards next time!

The final paddle

Chauffeur Derick with Eric

Some Questions raised by the Coast-to-Coast Walk

1. Why do they only put "C-to-C" signs where you don't need them?
2) Why do they make stiles so high and/or narrow?
3) Why is there always cow muck, even when there are no cows?
4) When there are cows, why do they choose the corner where the stile is as the major loo?
5) When there is all the countryside to go at, why does water choose to run on the path you're walking on?
6) Why don't screaming winds blow the mist away?
7) Why is the thing you want always in the other side pocket on the rucksack?
8) Why does anyone choose to live in Shap?
9) Why did we do the Coast-to-Coast in the wettest October in living memory?
10) Why did we do the Coast-to-Coast?

Our Coast-to-Coast tribute to J.J.

The sun and the rain
Gave joy and pain
The views we missed because of cloud
The views we saw that did us proud
All was worth it in the end
As our final tribute to our departed friend

for J.J.
R.I.P.

Eric and Lesley